EARLY TEXAS SCHOOLS

Early Texas Schools

A PHOTOGRAPHIC HISTORY

Text by Mary S. Black

Photographs by Bruce F. Jordan

UNIVERSITY OF TEXAS PRESS ⬮ AUSTIN

The publication of this book was generously supported by the Jess and Betty Jo Hay Endowment.

To S. I. Self, my grandfather, who rode to Thorp Springs, Texas, on a donkey to go to school. And to my aunt Louise Self, who taught high school biology for thirty years and never lost her love of the classroom.

—*Mary Black*

To my mother, Billie Adele Burroughs Jordan, who passed on her photographic genes and adventurous spirit.

To my grandmother, Neppie Lee Burroughs, who was a teacher herself and who was known as Miss Neppie to her students and the community of Sanger, Texas.

To my father, Burl Fowler Jordan, who shared his intelligence, sense of responsibility, and desire to know more of the world.

To my sister, Hilarie Lea Jordan Dzianott, because she is my sister, my source of strength and grounding.

To my son, Caleb Stephen Jordan, my traveling companion in this life and on these journeys.

—*Bruce Jordan*

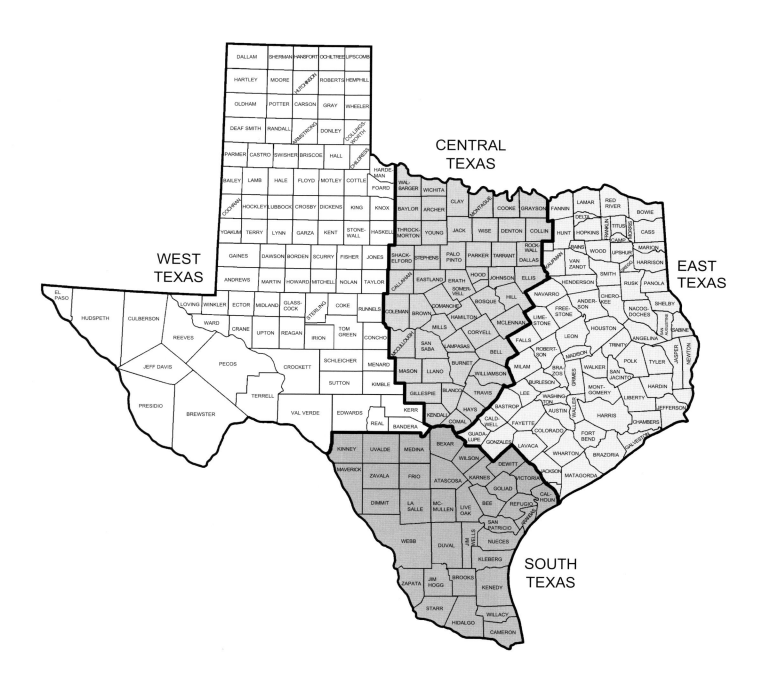

CENTRAL
TEXAS

WEST
TEXAS

EAST
TEXAS

SOUTH
TEXAS

DALLAM | SHERMAN | HANSFORT | OCHILTREE | LIPSCOMB
HARTLEY | MOORE | HUTCHINSON | ROBERTS | HEMPHILL
OLDHAM | POTTER | CARSON | GRAY | WHEELER
DEAF SMITH | RANDALL | ARMSTRONG | DONLEY | COLLINGS-WORTH
PARMER | CASTRO | SWISHER | BRISCOE | HALL | CHILDRESS
BAILEY | LAMB | HALE | FLOYD | MOTLEY | COTTLE | HARDE-MAN | FOARD
COCHRAN | HOCKLEY | LUBBOCK | CROSBY | DICKENS | KING | KNOX
YOAKUM | TERRY | LYNN | GARZA | KENT | STONE-WALL | HASKELL
GAINES | DAWSON | BORDEN | SCURRY | FISHER | JONES
ANDREWS | MARTIN | HOWARD | MITCHELL | NOLAN | TAYLOR
EL PASO
HUDSPETH | CULBERSON | LOVING | WINKLER | ECTOR | MIDLAND | GLASS-COCK | STERLING | COKE | RUNNELS
WARD | CRANE | UPTON | REAGAN | IRION | TOM GREEN | CONCHO
REEVES | PECOS | CROCKETT | SCHLEICHER | MENARD
JEFF DAVIS | SUTTON | KIMBLE
TERRELL
PRESIDIO | BREWSTER | VAL VERDE | EDWARDS | REAL | BANDERA | KERR

WAL-BARGER | WICHITA | CLAY | MONTAGUE | COOKE | GRAYSON | FANNIN | LAMAR | RED RIVER | BOWIE
BAYLOR | ARCHER | JACK | WISE | DENTON | COLLIN | HUNT | DELTA | FRANKLIN | TITUS | CAMP | MORRIS | CASS
THROCK-MORTON | YOUNG | PALO PINTO | PARKER | TARRANT | DALLAS | ROCK-WALL | KAUFMAN | RAINS | HOPKINS | WOOD | UPSHUR | MARION | HARRISON
SHACK-ELFORD | STEPHENS | VAN ZANDT | GREGG
CALLAHAN | EASTLAND | ERATH | HOOD | JOHNSON | ELLIS | NAVARRO | HENDERSON | SMITH | RUSK | PANOLA
COLEMAN | BROWN | COMANCHE | SOMER-VELL | BOSQUE | HILL | ANDER-SON | CHERO-KEE | NACOG-DOCHES | SHELBY
MCCULLOUGH | MILLS | HAMILTON | MCLENNAN | LIME-STONE | FREE-STONE | HOUSTON | TRINITY | ANGELINA | SAN AUGUSTINE | SABINE
SAN SABA | LAMPASAS | CORYELL | FALLS | LEON | POLK | TYLER | JASPER | NEWTON
MASON | LLANO | BURNET | WILLIAMSON | MILAM | ROBERT-SON | MADISON | WALKER | SAN JACINTO | HARDIN
GILLESPIE | BLANCO | TRAVIS | BRA-ZOS | BURLESON | GRIMES | MONT-GOMERY | LIBERTY
KENDALL | HAYS | BASTROP | LEE | WASHING-TON | WALLER | HARRIS | JEFFERSON
COMAL | CALD-WELL | FAYETTE | AUSTIN | CHAMBERS
GUADA-LUPE | GONZALES | COLORADO | FORT BEND | GALVESTON
KINNEY | UVALDE | MEDINA | BEXAR | WILSON | DEWITT | LAVACA | WHARTON | BRAZORIA
MAVERICK | ZAVALA | FRIO | ATASCOSA | KARNES | VICTORIA | JACKSON | MATAGORDA
DIMMIT | LA SALLE | MC-MULLEN | LIVE OAK | BEE | GOLIAD | REFUGIO | CAL-HOUN
WEBB | DUVAL | JIM WELLS | SAN PATRICIO | ARANSAS
NUECES
ZAPATA | JIM HOGG | BROOKS | KLEBERG
STARR | KENEDY
HIDALGO | WILLACY
CAMERON

This is the story of education in Texas, the first chapter so to speak. Like the state itself, this story is large, having many facets and characters just as diverse as the state. It can't all be told in one sitting. We're just telling the first part, from around 1850 to the 1930s.

As families moved into the new territory known as Texas, the first goal was to settle on the land and make it productive. What quickly followed was the desire for education for children, at least through the primary grades, before they had to help support the family.

Schools were built as they were needed and wherever someone donated the land. Some schools started in the shade of a large tree. Others began in dugouts. Families contributed wood for buildings if that was all they could afford. Even bachelor cowboys chipped in money. Simple one-room frame structures with pot-bellied stoves for heat served multiple purposes as schools, churches, community buildings, and dance halls, all in one.

In the early days, teachers often lived with families, moving from family to family throughout the year. The standard tenure for teachers was often only a year or two before they moved on to jobs with better pay and more stability.

"They [the Whiteflat School] had two cisterns. The janitor drew the water and poured it in a barrel. The barrel had three faucets, and you got your water that way."

C. D. Garrison, Matador, Texas

School districts did not exist until counties were organized. In 1891, Motley County, located in the Panhandle northeast of Lubbock, was organized. With the organization of the new county came the first school district in that area: Whiteflat. The district started with twenty students.

School attendance peaked in 1931 with 1703 students, and by 1939, there were 14 districts in Motley County. In 1972–1973, due to dropping enrollment and increased costs of operation, the districts consolidated, like many others before them. Today there is one district in the county, with one building and 165 students.

Small districts, 1-A's that graduate perhaps no more than ten to twelve students, are barely hanging on, but they persevere because of the tenacity and historical ties of the communities. Consolidation is inevitable, though, and this way of life will vanish soon into memory. When we look at some of the new secondary schools in Texas, large modern structures resembling college campuses built—in some cases—to educate over 2400 students, it is hard to remember the simple beginnings of education in Texas.

"I went to school there, as did my father. My father didn't graduate because students had to go to Pettus for twelfth grade and Pettus was too far to travel by horse."

John Goza, Normanna, Texas

My grandmother started teaching in San Angelo, Texas, before she moved to Sanger to raise a family. She was known as Miss Neppie to generations of students. As a child walking those hot, dusty summer streets in the mornings on the way to the grocery store with my grandmother, I would hear people call out, "Hello, Miss Neppie," and see them tip their hats. Those greetings set the tone for what would become my profession and passion in life: teaching and photographing the remains of former days.

—*Bruce F. Jordan*

We wish to thank all the people across the state of Texas who kindly took the time to tell us about their schools, communities, and lives. What a wonderful opportunity and adventure we had while traveling the road for this book! Many thanks to Dr. Frankie Monteverde, Dr. Rubén Garza, Dr. Sandra Wolf, Dr. Stephen L. Black, and Miles Sapp for their critical reading and good suggestions. And to Caleb Jordan—Bruce's patient son, traveling companion, partner in adventures, and navigator—and Steve Maikowski, for his long friendship, adventurous spirit, and professional support.

A dusty window reveals ancient textbooks piled on a desk inside a small frame structure overlooking the golden canyons of the Rio Grande. Inside, chalky blackboards and long-empty desks sit in silence. This used to be a school. In East Texas, a raw wind snaps an American flag over a red brick building as bare tree limbs rustle softly overhead. A tumble of clay blocks facing an overgrown field with a rusty swing set outlines the footprint of yet another building across town. Another façade, like a discarded Alamo, sits besieged by a sea of grass alone on the plains. Almost every town in Texas has at least one old school building such as these. Some are reused as museums or community centers, others are abandoned and deteriorating. Everywhere in Texas, parents built schools to educate the young, with hopeful hearts and high ambitions. Everywhere, children ran and shouted, played pranks, and recited their lessons for teachers. This is a story of early Texas schooling, and the buildings that stand as monuments to hope across the state.

This book chronicles education in Texas from its earliest beginnings to the era of the Great Depression through the images of school buildings across the state. The photographs by Bruce Jordan include some of the earliest known school facilities in Texas from the 1850s through some of the magnificent constructions of the oil boom in the 1930s. The story reflects the settlement of Texas, from the south and east toward the west and the High Plains. The characters include people from Mexico, Germany, Central Europe, the Old South, and elsewhere as they came to Texas to colonize, preach, or seek their fortunes. These groups approached the schooling of children in very different ways. Today, the old school buildings scattered across the state reflect these various ideas about educating the young and remind us how we arrived where we are today.

Early attempts in Texas to establish schools had mixed results: sometimes the schools closed quickly, sometimes they transformed into other institutions, and sometimes they lasted, a few even continuing to the present day. Many Texas communities were able to make public education a lasting reality after 1883, when the state legislature approved taxation to raise money for urban schools. By the 1920s, consolidation of

In 1965, President Lyndon B. Johnson signed the Elementary and Secondary Education Act in front of the Junction School on the Pedernales River near his ranch in Gillespie County. LBJ attended this school as a young boy.

rural schools began as people increasingly moved from the farm into town. The Gilmer-Aiken Laws in 1949 hastened further school consolidation as well as improved standards for teaching and class sizes. The federal Elementary and Secondary Education Act, passed in 1965 under Texas native President Lyndon Baines Johnson, completed the transformation of Texas public schools and others across the nation from small, segregated arrangements to the complex institutions prevalent today.

EARLY ATTEMPTS BY THE SPANISH

The first known instance of formal education in Texas began when Spanish missionaries sought to indoctrinate the indigenous peoples they found here in the late seventeenth century. The Spanish priests met with mixed success in teaching religion, language, agriculture, pottery-making, and stone masonry to the Native Americans. Evidence of their craft workshops can be found at Mission San José in San Antonio and Mission Nuestra Señora de Guadalupe in Goliad even today. Such teaching was not always welcomed, however. Attempts to convert the Apaches at Mission San Sabá ended in 1758 when the priests were murdered and the mission burned.

Following the missionaries, the Spanish colonists who founded San Antonio and Laredo during the eighteenth century soon gave thought to the education of juveniles in their midst. In Laredo in 1783, Don Santiago de Jesús Sánchez proclaimed that all colonial children of a certain age should attend school to learn to read and to pray, but this had no immediate effect in the young town. Soon thereafter in San Antonio de Béxar, Don Francisco de la Mata opened a school, claiming he was "much grieved of heart" at the condition of the children. He described them as "running about as vagabonds engaged only in pernicious pursuits such as playing with arrows and ropes, and spending their time in childish games and idle entertainments which lead only to perdition." Unfortunately, this school, along with other attempts to establish formal education during this era, produced only transitory results. In 1793 the king of

Spain mandated that public schools should be established in the North American colonies, but nothing was done in Texas. In 1802 the Spanish governor of Texas ordered compulsory school attendance for all colonial children under the age of twelve, but the order could not be enforced due to a lack of teachers and reluctance on the part of the children and their families.

By 1821 the Laredo city council received a petition from José Lázaro Benavides to teach children to read and write. Apparently his job duties included teaching good behavior to the students as well as academics. The city council noted that:

It shall be his duty to guard the conduct of the children both in and out of school, making them understand in a clear manner the veneration and respect they owe to the public authorities, their parents, old persons, and elders; also that they shall be careful with the cleanliness of speech, deportment and good conduct.

Parents paid Benavides a small sum every month for each beginning student, and somewhat more for advanced students who were learning to write. If parents did not have the money, Benavides would take beef or corn in trade. His efforts produced moderate results, and by 1822 there was a school for boys in Laredo that taught both logic and civics.

Near the Mexican border, there was also a tradition of so-called "dame" schools during this period and continuing until at least the 1960s. Cultured women conducted small private schools in their homes, teaching children how to read and write and also how to behave in polite society. Lessons were generally conducted in Spanish and often included instruction in music, embroidery, or other arts. An old residential building that formerly served as a dame school is now the Head Start Center[1] in Hebbronville. The center stands directly across the street from the towering Catholic church and seminary for Mexican priests, a reminder of the intertwined history of Texas and Mexico.

Even though various formal attempts to teach children and indigenous peoples were made during the period when Texas belonged to Spain, Spanish influence on schooling was minimal, except for the continuance of dame schools. Texas became part of Mexico in 1821 when Mexico won independence from Spain, and it was soon open to colonists from the United States. With them came new ideas about education.

STEPHEN F. AUSTIN'S COLONY AND THE REPUBLIC

Pioneer children from the United States in Austin's first colony learned their ABCs around the family hearth in the cabins of San Felipe de Austin, located near the Brazos River in present-day Washington County. With the arrival of

Thomas Pilgrim in 1829, the first known English-speaking teacher in Texas, such simple schooling changed. Pilgrim taught the children of Stephen F. Austin's colony the four R's: readin', ritin', 'rithmetic, and religion. Presbyterian minister P. H. Fullenwider joined the colony a few years later to continue the work Pilgrim began. The Mexican state of Coahuila y Tejas, to which the colony belonged, required the establishment of primary schools and made land grants to support local schools in the 1830s with limited results. In other settlements of Austin's colony, Frances Trask Thompson opened a boarding school for girls in Coles' Settlement (later renamed Independence) in 1834, and Lydia Ann McHenry opened two short-lived schools in Washington County during the next few years. A school survey in 1834 lists several schools outside Austin's colony in San Antonio, near the coast in Brazoria, and in East Texas in Nacogdoches and San Augustine.

The men who wrote the Texas Declaration of Independence in 1836 were not satisfied with these sporadic efforts. Among their grievances against Mexico was the charge that Mexico

has failed to establish any public system of education, although possessed of almost boundless resources, and although it is an axiom in political science, that unless a people are educated and enlightened, it is idle to expect the continuance of civil liberty, or the capacity for self-government.

When Mirabeau B. Lamar was elected the second president of Texas in 1839, he reminded the Congress of the Republic that "[a] cultivated mind is the guardian genius of democracy," and encouraged the legislature to set aside public lands to endow a public school system and two universities. This advocacy earned him the nickname of "The Father of Texas Education"; nonetheless, public financing of schools did not take root in the Republic. Private schools like Rutersville College near La Grange, Miss A. E. Madden's Female Academy in San Augustine, and the Matagorda Academy for both boys and girls established by Rev. and Mrs. C. S. Ives remained the norm during the 1840s.

Statehood in 1846 encouraged a new wave of immigrants into Texas from Europe and the United States. Educated people from Germany, France, Poland, and elsewhere brought their knowledge to the frontier and helped the new state prosper. The Masonic Order worked aggressively to organize local schools and promote a general state educational system. Christian educators began to establish local universities, colleges, and academies. Some people believed in schools conducted by churches but endowed and

Nacogdoches University was chartered in 1845 under the Republic of Texas. The red brick Greek Revival building which stands today was built in 1858 and used as a hospital during the Civil War. The building was deeded to the Nacogdoches Independent School District in 1904 and is currently used as a museum.

paid for by the state. Others were either indifferent or wholly opposed to using state wealth to support schools. Many Anglo Americans thought that education should be entirely a family matter; intervention by the state was considered by some Texans to be an affront to personal dignity.

GERMAN IMMIGRANTS BRING NEW EXPECTATIONS

When German settlers arrived in Texas in the mid-1840s, however, they brought with them progressive ideas about education that were prevalent in Germany at the time. The teachers were often trained in German universities and brought their high academic standards to the Texas frontier. One of the first teachers was Hermann Seele, who settled in New Braunfels. He conducted his first class under a giant oak tree in 1845, teaching reading and singing to the village children in their native tongue. A modest building used for church services on Sunday and school during the week was built the following year, allowing learning to continue in cold or rainy weather. Tragedy struck the new immigrants that same year, however, when illness (possibly cholera) killed many newly arrived German adults at Indianola[2] but left their children untouched. An orphanage was

Vereins-Kirche.

quickly established near the Guadalupe River, where the children were not only cared for, but also were given lessons in fundamental academic subjects. Education continued to flourish in New Braunfels, which boasted a library of over two thousand volumes by 1857.

In 1847 German settlers moved to the Fredericksburg area and built the Vereins-Kirche (or Society Church). The building was nicknamed the Kaffeemühle (coffee mill) because of its shape, a distinct German style known as a Carolingian octagon. Instruction for the pioneer children was held during the week in the Vereins-Kirche for about ten years under the leadership of Johann Leyendecker. Leyendecker and others taught in German, and children mostly used textbooks their parents had brought with them from the old country. Fifty years after the original Vereins-Kirche was built, it became so weather-damaged that it was torn down. The building was replaced with an exact replica of the original to celebrate the Texas Centennial in 1936. This unique Texas building stands in the center of town today as a beacon to tourists flocking to experience Fredericksburg's Old World charm.

After 1856, when English instruction was required in addition to German, children often wrote bilingual lessons, with English on one side of the notebook and German on the other. In New Braunfels, students in the lower class were required to study reading and writing, arithmetic, natural history and science, geography and history, essay writing, public speaking, recitation, and singing. Private schools also flourished, such as the German Free School in Austin, which opened in 1858. Despite the name, the families of young scholars paid to enroll their children. In fact, so many students enrolled that a second story was added to the building a few years later, with the construction work carried out after class by the enterprising teacher, Julius Schütze.

One of the customs brought to Texas by the Germans was "Schulpruefung," a final exam day celebrated with school picnics and entertainment that continues even today in certain Hill Country communities. School-closing celebrations included barbecue, plays, and dances. Before the festivities could begin, however, the students had to submit to examination in front of the gathered families and community members. The county judge or a neighboring teacher often administered oral exams to the young scholars. At other times, the parents asked the examination questions. Spelling bees and speed exercises in math also demonstrated the skills learned during the school term. This public display created a certain amount of anxiety for the teacher as well as for the students.

After the questioning, it was time for fun. Succulent barbecue slow-roasted in deep pits dug in the ground was traditionally served, along with potato salad, sauerkraut, coleslaw, and Jell-O salads. Dinners were sold to make money for the school, and admission was charged for the plays and dances. Students were given two or three free tickets for drinks or ice cream as a treat. Adults in the community often presented plays in the evening, in English or German. Dances were also popular and sometimes lasted until the wee hours. If the

Spelling Lessons from Gillespie County at the Turn of the Twentieth Century

Rat, bat, mat
Man, ran, fan
Fat, pat, sat
Lap, map, nap
Sad, had, bad

Spelling Lesson 208
Babel, Babble
Cable, cabal
Choral, coral
Carnal, charnel
Caldron, chaldron
Brought, borrow
Gesture, jester
Umbel, humble
Accept, except
Leaven, eleven
Pelisse, police

school did not raise enough money for improvements and repairs this way, the parents paid the rest out-of-pocket.

Today, twelve country schoolhouses built by German Texans still stand in Gillespie County, monuments to the early settlers' belief in education. Lyndon B. Johnson, later president of the United States, attended the Albert School near Williams Creek and the Junction School on the Pedernales River in Gillespie County in the early 1920s. His father, Sam Ealy Johnson Jr., had been the schoolmaster at the one-room Rocky School in neighboring Blanco County in 1896. President Johnson returned to the picturesque Junction School to sign the Elementary and Secondary Education Act of 1965, with his former teacher by his side. This legislation was the most sweeping federal involvement in American education ever created. Today, No Child Left Behind, signed in 2002, updates and incorporates many of these same goals.

"The Great Society is a place where every child can find knowledge to enrich his mind and to enlarge his talents."

Lyndon B. Johnson

THE FRENCH ANSWER THE BISHOP'S CALL

San Antonio experienced a certain amount of French influence during the 1850s with the arrival of several Alsatian priests and French Catholic nuns. Catholic bishop Jean-Marie Odin recognized the need for a school and organized a group of seven nuns from the French Catholic Ursuline Order and four Marianist brothers to open separate schools for girls and boys in the city. "A good school alone will be able to generate the people since the city is swarming with children plunged in the depths of ignorance," the bishop declared.

The Ursuline sisters determined to open their school in a partially finished *pise de terre* (or "rammed earth") building constructed by the French architects Francois Giraud and Jules Poinsard, who both lived in San Antonio at the time. The construction process involved compressing rock, straw, and native clay by hand. The first building was a bit leaky when the school opened on November 2, 1851, but it had a lovely, ten-acre site overlooking the San Antonio River. After 115 years at this location, the sisters moved the academy to northwest San Antonio. The buildings of the old Ursuline Academy now house the Southwest School of Art and Craft, a showpiece on the scenic River Walk.

The Marianist brothers opened their first school for boys with twelve students on August 25, 1852, in two rooms over a livery stable near San Fernando Cathedral. The school was so popular that by Christmas, more than one hundred students were enrolled. By March of 1853, the brothers opened a new two-story school building

Ursuline Gate, 1851.

called St. Mary's Institute on a small piece of land on the San Antonio River. The remains of the original building are incorporated today into a River Walk hotel. St. Mary's has undergone many changes in the past one hundred and fifty years, but the present configurations of St. Mary's University (1927) and Central Catholic High School (1852) continue in a direct line from this early venture.

Two nuns from the Sisters of Divine Providence arrived in Texas from France in 1866 to open a school in Austin. They, and others who later joined them, also taught school in Castroville, Corpus Christi, Danville, D'Hanis, Fredericksburg, Frelsburg, New Braunfels, Panna Maria, and St. Hedwig. In 1994, almost two hundred sisters from this order worked in Texas schools, hospitals, and clinics.

Besides the Germans and French, immigrants from other European countries also found their way to Texas. When Polish settlers first arrived in 1855, they taught their children at home. In 1868, however, these immigrants established a formal school in Panna Maria in Karnes County. The oldest private Polish school in America, it still stands today. Other immigrants from Central Europe established the Moravia School and the Velehrad School in Lavaca County prior to the Civil War, and classes were conducted primarily in Czech until 1895. These two rural schools consolidated with Halletsville schools in 1972. Settlers from Denmark arrived in Texas in 1895 and formed the town of Danevang in Wharton County. The Dansk Folkesamfund (Danish People's Society) soon set up a school for children to learn Danish history and language. Immigrants from Norway and Sweden also contributed to the educational legacy in Texas. For example, Palm Elementary School in Austin was named after the Swedish immigrant Swante Palm, who was a member of the city council.

SETTLERS FROM THE UNITED STATES

Besides Europeans, people from other areas of the United States also showed an interest in educating the young in the new state of Texas. Education was a prominent component of Presbyterian evangelism and a central concern for missionary Melinda Rankin when she came to Texas to teach Spanish-speaking students and share her religious message. She opened a school for Hispanic girls in Brownsville in 1852, which later became the Rio Grande Female Institute. The curriculum focused on English and intensive Biblical studies. Rankin's school in Brownsville competed with Villa Maria, a Catholic girls' school founded by the Ursulines, also in 1852. The Chappell Hill Institute, founded in Washington County in 1850 for both men and women, came under the sponsorship of the Methodist Church by 1854 and remained open until 1912. The Austin Collegiate Female Institute offered a broad curriculum to young ladies in 1852, with different fees for different courses of study. For twenty-five dollars, a scholar could enjoy lessons in logic; botany; natural, mental, and moral philosophy; chemistry; geography of the heavens; algebra; plane and spherical geometry; trigonometry; and Latin, Greek, or Hebrew. French, Spanish, waxwork, shellwork, and music were available for an extra fee.

Several schools for boys were also opened during this time in Waco. T. N. Sneed, the first known schoolmaster in Waco, operated a school in 1851. The Trinity River Male High School opened in 1855 and became known as Waco University in 1861. This institution subsequently was folded into Baylor University.

Prior to the Civil War, disabled students

The Asylum for the Blind opened in Austin before the Civil War as the forerunner of the Texas School for the Blind and Visually Impaired. The building is now part of the University of Texas campus, located near highway I-35.

learned vocational training and basic life skills at the Asylum for the Blind (now the Texas School for the Blind and Visually Impaired), which opened in Austin in 1856, and the Institution for the Deaf and Dumb (now Texas School for the Deaf), which opened in the capital city the following year. Three students attended the blind asylum the first year, and eleven students came to the deaf school, but enrollments quickly grew as word spread of this opportunity.

In 1854 Governor Elisha M. Pease established a permanent school fund of two million dollars, creating the fiscal foundation for modern Texas public schools. Although few public schools resulted directly from this action, San Antonio established a public school district in response to the governor's initiative. The Civil War soon disrupted life throughout Texas, however, and little progress in education was made until the conflict ended.

Schooling was not the most pressing concern in the state immediately after the Civil War. For example, the Academy of the Sacred Heart opened in Waco in 1873 to low attendance. The diary of one sister for opening day read: "Wednesday, opening of the school and not one pupil came. Thursday, three Episcopalians and one Catholic came."

Several cities with established schools, such as Fredericksburg, Houston, and San Antonio, were large enough to receive aid from the Peabody Fund after the Civil War. Northern philanthropist George Peabody wanted to encourage the growth of schools in the Old South. Conditions for this aid required an enrollment of one hundred students or more and a daily attendance of at least eighty-five, a standard that few communities in Texas could meet at that time.

The 1850 Texas census showed that most white men and women in Texas could read and write to some degree, despite limited schooling opportunities. For the almost sixty thousand enslaved people of African heritage in Texas, however, learning to read and write was generally forbidden by their masters, with rare exceptions.

The census notes 397 free blacks in the state at that time, but only 217 of them could read. Although a few slaves may have been taught the basics, literate blacks were uncommon due to the suppression of education for blacks throughout the South.

There is only meager evidence of schooling for blacks in Texas before the Civil War. Research suggests that a Methodist Church in Houston housed a school for black students at least briefly in the 1850s. Near Carthage in East Texas, a rudimentary school existed by Bird Holland's plantation. Holland was one of the founders of Carthage in Panola County; he later served as Texas secretary of state. Around 1850 he freed three slaves, James, Milton, and William Holland—possibly his sons—and sent them to school in Ohio, which had a liberal policy toward people of African heritage. After the Civil War, former slaves established the community of Holland Quarters a few miles from the plantation. Black children learned to read and write in Holland Quarters until 1969, when the students and teachers transferred to the public schools in Carthage Independent School District.

After the Civil War, the Freedmen's Bureau (1865–1870) established schools in Texas for newly freed slaves. By some estimates, 150 Freedmen's Bureau Schools were opened by 1870, including day schools, night schools, and Sabbath schools. Educated blacks from outside Texas held about half of the teaching positions in these schools by the time the Freedmen's Bureau ceased operations in Texas. Many educators at the Freedmen's Bureau Schools tried to make the most of the new opportunity for education by providing an ambitious curriculum including arithmetic, reading, writing, history, geography, civics, politics, home economics, and vocational training.

Possibly the first school in Texas attended by both black and white children was at Meusebach Creek in Gillespie County. In 1869 the Washington children—Henry, Laura, Minnie, Ovie, and George—whose parents were freed slaves, attended this school alongside students of German heritage, whose parents had generally favored the Union during the Civil War. Germans in the Fredericksburg area were harassed for their stand with the Union, and a teacher named Louis Schütze was hanged by Confederate vigilantes during the strife.

In 1869, the Freedman's Bureau built a two-story stone structure on Rincon Street[3] in San Antonio, the largest city in the state at that time, to provide instruction for black students of all ages. Two years later, the city, which also had five free public schools for white children, assumed operation of the school. San Antonio continued to expand its educational offerings by opening its first high school for white students in 1879. The white high school later became known as Fox Tech High School, and it continues to serve students today. The original black school became known as the Frederick Douglass School around 1902. Black students were first offered a high school curriculum at the Douglass school in 1914, when it relocated to a new, two-story brick building, now on Martin Luther King Drive. Ten years later, San Antonio continued to lead educational progress in the state by restructuring its secondary schools to include junior high school. The first junior high school for black children in Texas was held at the Douglass school. From 1969 to 1999, the Douglass school served students of all races as an integrated elementary school. The Rincon Street Douglass school had provided the keys to learning for children for 130 years when the building was closed for renovation in 2003.

The Texas Constitution of 1876 specifically called for separate schools for white and "colored" children, a situation that prevailed until the mid-1950s, when a few school districts began to obey the 1954 Supreme Court ruling for integrated schools in *Brown v. Board of Education*. Many schools for black students that opened shortly after Reconstruction took a variety of forms and had long-lasting effects in the communities they served. Ms. Myrtle Moses Mathis taught black students in her home in Gonzales County in the 1870s. By 1890 the school had enlarged to fill a two-story building. A brick schoolhouse was built in 1914, and the school was named George Edwards High School in 1922. By 1940 there were three hundred

The Frederick Douglass School is a direct descendant of the first Freedman's Bureau School for African Americans in San Antonio.

students and eight teachers. The school continued in operation for almost one hundred years, until school integration brought about its closure in 1964.[4] In Seguin, the Second Baptist Church sponsored the first school for blacks in a frame building called the Lincoln School. In 1892 the Lincoln School became part of the Seguin public school system, and in 1925 the name was changed to Ball High School in honor of Reverend William Baton Ball, the first principal. This school, along with other historically black schools, closed in 1966, due to the achievement of integration of black and white children.

Opportunities for education for blacks beyond the fundamentals of basic literacy were also introduced into Texas soon after the Civil War. The African Methodist Episcopal Church in Austin founded Paul Quinn College as the first black college in the state in 1872. Five men and women on the first faculty taught mathematics, Latin, theology, English, printing, carpentry, blacksmithing, leather tanning, saddle making, "kitchen and dining room work," and other skills. Paul Quinn continues to serve students on its Dallas campus today, as it has for over 130 years. Its sister college is Wiley College in Marshall, which was started by the Freedmen's Aid Society of the Methodist Episcopal Church in 1873. White men served as administrators and teachers at Wiley College until 1892, when most of the four hundred black students withdrew in protest. Bishop Isaiah B. Scott, a former slave and graduate of Central Tennessee College, was hired as president along with several black teachers as a result of this protest.

The federal Morrill Land-Grant College Acts made land grant colleges possible in numerous states after the Civil War. The Morrill Acts resulted in two institutions in race-segregated Texas: the Agricultural and Mechanical College of Texas (now Texas A&M University) and Prairie View College (now Prairie View A&M University). Thus, in 1878, Prairie View became the first public college for blacks in the state. Perhaps symbolically, the college was originally housed in a stately, two-story, white plantation home with tall columns and double porches overlooking the grounds. The plantation's mistress had once operated a fashionable girls' school in the home. Administration of the college was quickly turned over to black educators, including the brothers E. H. and L. C. Anderson, and later Edward L. Blackshear and I. M. Terrell, all four of whom influenced Texas public education for many years. L. C. Anderson later organized the Colored Teachers State Association of Texas, which led efforts for advanced education and fair treatment of black students and teachers. Several historically black public schools throughout the state carry the names of these men in commemoration of their achievements.

Most early black schools were continually underfunded and were forced to find creative ways to exist. Students at Tillotson College in Austin literally took matters into their own hands when they built the Old Administration Building, as it is now called, brick by brick. Construction took three years and was partially funded by humble five- and ten-cent contributions from blacks living in the vicinity. Tillotson opened as a private school in 1881, founded by the American

"Prairie View A&M University is an institution. But an institution is an empty thing without the beating hearts of yearning souls of mortal men. And down through the 120 years of Prairie View's existence, men have lived and dreamed here until every blade of grass and every rock in that wise primordial way in which the primitive earth knows and cares, has joined the choir invisible to bless their memory."

Excerpt from a speech by Dr. George R. Woolfolk on the seventy-fifth anniversary of Prairie View A&M University

15

Missionary Association and affiliated with the United Church of Christ and the United Methodist Church. In 1952, it merged with another black school, Huston College, when highway construction demolished the Huston campus. Today, the Old Administration Building is considered a rare example of historic African American architecture and construction.

Mary Allen Seminary for Colored Girls opened its doors in Crockett in 1886 and served the region for ninety-two years until closing in 1978. The school was founded by the Board of Missions for Freedmen of the Presbyterian Church. Mary E. Allen, wife of the first white principal, raised a considerable sum to help finance the school. When she died shortly before the campus opened, the school was named for her. The campus eventually had twelve buildings, including dormitories, landscaped gardens, and a fountain. There was a succession of white male presidents until 1925, when Byrd R. Smith became the first black man to head the institution. Dr. Smith hired more black faculty and quickly increased enrollment to 134 students, all of whom lived in the dormitories. During this period, Texas had 150 institutions offering one or more years of high school for blacks, including fourteen city high schools, six county high schools, and high school departments in every junior and senior college for blacks.

In 1933 Dr. Smith led the campaign for the school's change in status from a seminary to a co-educational junior college accredited by the State Department of Education. This accreditation allowed students to receive teaching certificates, thus giving them better job opportunities and greater mobility. The college lost this accreditation twenty years later, however, due to a scandal involving the sale of academic credentials. In 1961 Hurricane Carla tore the roof off the main administration building and caused extensive damage. The school finally closed in 1978 when maintenance and funding issues forced the point. Today, the ruins stand as a haunting reminder of the dreams and determination of Mary Allen's former students.

THE EDUCATION EXPLOSION OF THE
LATE NINETEENTH CENTURY

The bitterness of the Civil War and Reconstruction eras gradually gave way to hopes of greater prosperity for Texas. The final decades of the nineteenth century saw three major developments in education in the state: the swift increase in public elementary and secondary schools, the first signs of the kindergarten movement, and the establishment of universities.

The question of free public schools for everyone encountered heavy opposition at first and was eloquently described years later by a school principal in Waco, known only as Mr. Gallagher:

The antagonism of the Reconstruction Period was not

yet passed [by 1880]. *The attitude of many people was distinctly hostile toward any system of public free schools. There was a decided reluctance on the part of many people to pay school taxes to educate the masses of illiterate Negro children. There was also a number of people who objected*
and refused to send their children to public schools simply because they were free. To them patronage of such schools carried the intimation that they were accepting charity.

Miss Lizzie Highston, a member of the first graduating class of Waco High School in 1887, later described people's evolving sentiment regarding these schools:

The public schools took over several of the private schools and gradually employed most of the teachers. My father had the point of view, typical of those days, that only the "riff-raff" attended them. He allowed his two boys to go but was firm in his conviction that a free school was no place for a girl. By 1883, however, the tide was turning in favor of public schools.

By 1883 the legislature began to believe that good schools would help the economy and that money spent on schools was better than money spent on alternatives such as jails and penitentiaries. Legislation passed that year allowing taxation in urban areas for community schools, which resulted in a flurry of school-building activity. Today, many towns, such as Denton, Midland, and San Angelo, date their free public schools to this period.

Around the turn of the twentieth century, middle-class, educated white women began to demonstrate concern about child labor and illiteracy all across the United States.

This was a period of intensive immigration from southern Europe and elsewhere, as well as rapid industrialization and urbanization, all of which created enormous change throughout the country, including in Texas. The first example of this public concern for child welfare in the state occurred in El Paso with a dynamic woman named Olga Bernstein Kohlberg. She immigrated to Texas in 1875 from Germany, where the kindergarten movement began. In 1891 she organized the Child Culture Study Circle, a group of local women who promoted the education of young children, and, two years later, she successfully convinced the El Paso Board of Education to establish the first kindergarten in the state. Her further work as a philanthropist and civic activist included organizing

Schoolbooks Used in Texas around the Turn of the Twentieth Century

Wentworth, G. A. 1904. *The First Steps in Algebra*. Am M. Ginn & Co.

Swinton, William. 1872. *Swinton's First Lessons in Our Country's History*. American Book Company.

Hunt, J. N., and H. I. Gourley. 1896. *The Modern Spelling Book*. Sheldon & Co., price 18¢.

Tarr, R. S. 1903. *New Physical Geography*. The MacMillian Co., price 88¢.

Triplett, H. F., and F. A. Hauslein. 1912. *Civics: Texas and Federal*. Rein & Sons Co., price 75¢.

the first hospital and first library in the city. Shortly after Mrs. Kohlberg's example, the Dallas Free Kindergarten Training and Industrial Association established Neighborhood House, a settlement house that offered services to poor immigrants. A free kindergarten opened in Dallas around 1900 and enrolled about one hundred children from Russian Jewish immigrant families.

Settlement houses sprang up in poor neighborhoods of most Texas cities at the beginning of the new century, and with them free kindergartens. Bethlehem House in Houston offered kindergarten to African American youngsters during this period. Rusk House in Houston, Inman House in San Antonio, and Houchen Settlement in Segundo Barrio in El Paso provided services for children of Mexican heritage. Sybil Campbell and the Houston Women's Club also participated in this trend of educating children at a young age. Kindergartens were often sponsored by Methodist institutions called Wesley Houses in various cities. Businesses such as the cotton mills in Bonham and South Dallas found that providing kindergarten for female workers' children enabled them to keep enough employees for profitable production. Kindergartens were fairly common by the time Jovita Idar, the first president of the League of Mexican Women, established one in San Antonio in the 1920s. The kindergarten movement had spread throughout the state.

THE GROWTH OF UNIVERSITIES

Today, white columns shaded by ancient live oaks overlook low stone ruins in Washington County near Independence as reminders of the first buildings of Baylor University. Sponsored by the Baptist Church, Baylor has been in continuous operation since it was incorporated under the laws of the Republic of Texas in 1845. Baylor is the oldest institution of higher learning in Texas still operating under its original name. The remaining columns mark the Baylor Female Department, which later moved to Belton and became the University of Mary Hardin-Baylor. On a hill to the south, across a stream known as "The River Jordan" to the students, young men attended Baylor University. Classes were held there until 1886, when the university consolidated with Waco University to become present-day Baylor.

Austin College in Sherman is the oldest Presbyterian college in the state, founded in 1849 in Huntsville. Twenty years later, Presbyterians folded three small schools into Trinity University in the town of Tehuacana, where there were three churches, two combination grist mills/

The Bachelor Girls' Library Club was formed by fifteen young women in 1902 to promote the public library in Rusk. In 1904, they rescinded a rule against married members and changed the name to "The Maids and Matrons Library Club" to include several members who had recently married. They eventually contributed more than 23,000 books to the city library.

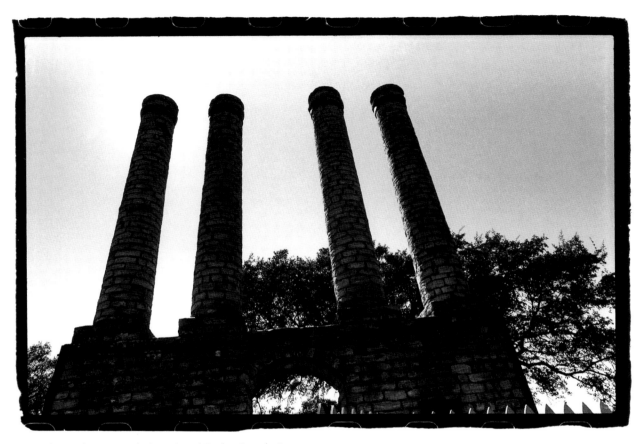

Four white columns mark the original Baylor Female Department.

cotton gins, and about five hundred residents after the Civil War. An impressive four-story building of locally cut limestone was constructed around 1871 in a predominantly Second Empire style with Gothic details and a mansard roof. Trinity operated in this location until 1902, when it moved to Waxahachie; it later settled in San Antonio.

Texas took advantage of the Morrill Land-Grant College Acts after the Civil War when the legislature authorized the first state-governed institution of higher learning in 1871, partly to encourage economic recovery from the hostilities. When the Texas Agricultural and Mechanical College (Texas A&M University) opened its doors in 1876 to the first 106 students and six faculty, courses in clas-

"Pro Ecclesia, Pro Texana"
Motto of Baylor University

sics, literature, and applied mathematics prevailed. Three years later, strong protests from farmers in the state caused the removal of the first president and faculty and installed an all-new administration along with a mandated curriculum in agriculture and engineering. In addition, the all-male college included compulsory military training, and for many years, it graduated more regularly commissioned military officers than any other institution in the United States.

Benefiting thousands of new students during the post–Civil War period, teaching itself became more professional as new organizations to advocate for instructors and students were formed. The Texas State Teachers Association (TSTA) was formed in 1880 when two smaller groups joined forces to promote the advancement of education. One of the early successes of the organization was its formulation of a plan for a state-supported university. In 1881 Governor Oran M. Roberts closely followed the TSTA recommendations in an exhortation to the legislature, which resulted in the formation of the University of Texas.

The University of Texas at Austin opened the doors of knowledge to its first students in 1883 in the west wing of Old Main, the first building constructed on the forty-acre campus. The first year saw 221 young men and women sign up for advanced work under eight professors. The university offered coeducational classes in liberal arts, science, and law. It also fostered the growth of high schools throughout the state in order to prepare students for advanced academic training. Austin and many other cities opened their first public high schools at this same time. UT served as the accreditation agency for high school course work for the state, certifying the rigor of secondary school courses appropriate for college preparation. In 1923, oil was discovered on university land in West Texas, spurring a construction boom on campus that lasted through the Great Depression. The original Victorian Gothic Old Main was torn down, giving way to beautiful Spanish Renaissance architecture and the iconic present-day tower in its place. With the establishment of Texas A&M and the University of Texas, the realization of Mirabeau B. Lamar's 1839 dream of two universities in Texas was complete.

Larissa College was established in a log cabin in Cherokee County in 1848. After moving to a new building around 1855, it boasted the latest equipment, including perhaps the most powerful telescope in the South, and offered the strongest science training available at that time in Texas. The school closed as a result of the Civil War.

"Disciplina Praesidium Civitatis"
Motto of the University of Texas

EARLY TWENTIETH-CENTURY GROWTH

Although the first three decades of the twentieth century saw many attempts at school improvement in Texas, much was left to be desired. New laws that allowed bonds for common school construction in 1905 and 1909 precipitated the founding of many new schools throughout the state during this time. Education became compulsory shortly before World War I, and an organized movement for enhanced schooling was promoted in newspapers and during political rallies. Opportunities for black children and children of Mexican heritage also expanded through a variety of means. More Texans began to receive college educations as well, as universities continued to expand throughout the state.

School attendance at primary and secondary schools was sporadic until the Compulsory School Act of 1915. A Houston superintendent complained of only a 71 percent attendance rate in 1910, but he attributed this to muddy streets from heavy rains. By 1916 all children between the ages of eight and fourteen were required to attend school at least three months per year. This requirement increased to five months two years later. School districts wishing to offer more days of schooling had to find the additional funds necessary to pay teachers from the local community.

In truth, the Compulsory School Act was only loosely enforced and was often overlooked altogether for black children and children of Mexican heritage. For example, the new Metz Elementary School in Austin enrolled at least one child of Mexican descent in 1917, but several hundred others who were not enrolled were actually on the census records for that neighborhood. Short school terms and incidental attendance in many communities adversely affected the academic achievement of black and Hispanic children in the state until the 1960s.

Professor W. S. Sutton of the University of Texas and newspaper editor Clarence N. Ousley of the *Fort Worth Record* led an intensive campaign for better schools, which resulted in the ability to collect taxes for rural schools as well as urban ones. A statewide Conference for Education in 1907 focused attention on school issues. In 1918, with the ratification of the women's suffrage amendment to the U.S. Constitution just around the corner, Annie Webb Blanton became the first woman elected to any state office when she won the position of state superintendent of public instruction. In 1918, women had won the right to vote in Texas primaries and exercised their voting rights for the first time that July. Blanton defeated the incumbent by a large margin and went on to win handily in the November election. She served as state superintendent for two terms, advocating for better schools by raising teachers'

The first football game between the University of Texas and Texas A&M ended in a UT victory, 38–0, in 1894.

Boys' Corn Clubs and Girls' Tomato Clubs

Starting around 1908 in Jack County, Boys' Corn Clubs and Girls' Tomato Clubs enjoyed considerable popularity among adolescents in rural Texas. Mrs. Edna Westbrook Trigg, a high school principal, introduced Cameron County to Girls' Tomato Clubs in 1912. These social and agricultural organizations focused on proper growing and canning techniques and were forerunners of today's 4-H Clubs.

Three books—the Instructor's School Library.

salaries, improving textbooks, and removing state constitutional obstructions to tax rates for local school districts.

Even though Blanton was a strong leader in Texas public education, she did little to promote schooling for black or non-English-speaking children. Growth in educational opportunities for black students in Texas during the 1920s was primarily due to the influence and money of several philanthropic institutions located in northern states rather than to the efforts of the state of Texas itself. Spanish-speaking refugees, who poured over the border during the Mexican Revolution of 1910–1920, found schools in Texas unprepared to accept them.

NORTHERN PHILANTHROPY EXPANDS EDUCATIONAL DREAMS

Julius Rosenwald was the president and later chairman of Sears, Roebuck & Company, head-quartered in Chicago. From his personal fortune, he gave generously to various charities. His acquaintance with Booker T. Washington, founder and president of the Tuskegee Institute in Alabama, led to the idea of challenge grants for elementary schools serving black children. The Rosenwald Fund was the most prolific contributor to black schools in Texas during the 1920s and 1930s, providing challenge grants for the construction of more than 464 schools, teachers' homes, and industrial training shops in 78 counties. Overall, the Rosenwald Fund helped build nearly five thousand schools for blacks throughout the South, educating almost a third of all black children in school at the time.

Many of the so-called Rosenwald schools were built in communities established by freedmen after the Civil War. The buildings were often constructed with volunteer labor from fathers and mothers seeking a better life for their children. Communities held covered-dish suppers and baseball games to raise money for the matching funds. Some sharecroppers set aside an area of cotton, commonly known as the "Rosenwald Patch," as their contribution. In some cases, local tax money was also available for these projects.

Two professors at the Tuskegee Institute created a series of architectural plans for Rosenwald schools. Schools had from one to seven rooms, which were often divided by sliding doors that could open to form a larger space for performances and plays. Many schools had a raised wooden stage. Two-story buildings had separate stairways for boys and girls. Windows had to face east/west to get the most natural light, and each school site was required to provide at least two acres for playgrounds, sports fields, and garden plots.

During this period Sears and Roebuck sold mail-order home-building kits, including all plans and materials, delivered to the customer by wagon or train. There is a story from Gillespie County of a teacher who ordered a home-building kit from Sears, which he then erected near the school as a teacherage. When he took another job, he moved and took the house with him! The value of standardized plans was apparent to the company, and they aggressively marketed Rosenwald plans to administrators and school boards for white schools as well. Eventually, almost fifteen thousand white schools were built throughout the country from the standardized architectural plans first conceived at the Tuskegee Institute to serve rural black children.

Teacher Evaluations in 1914

In his 1914 evaluation of Austin public schools, E. D. Jennings rated a teacher as excellent if she was "beautiful, properly dressed, and had a proper voice." She was rated as poor if she was determined to be "sickly and improperly dressed [and spoke] with a harsh voice." Instruction itself was not rated.

TEXAS
First in size.
First in agricultural products.
First in production of cotton.
First in production of oil.
Seventh in wealth.
Thirty-ninth in education.
Shall Texas keep this rank?

Slogan for the Better Schools Campaign, 1919–1923

Sweet Home Rosenwald School in Guadalupe County.

An example of such a school still stands in Sweet Home in Guadalupe County. Guadalupe County had six Rosenwald schools, and land for the Sweet Home School was donated by German immigrant William M. Stein. Sweet Home also had a county training school funded by the Slater Foundation that taught eighth grade and such skills as cooking and sewing, vocational agriculture, blacksmithing, mattress making, and auto mechanics. By 1933, Sweet Home was touted as the "outstanding black community in the nation" by *Farm and Ranch Magazine*. Schools in Texas communities like this one prepared black youth to lead more prosperous lives than their parents had led, and sometimes also prepared them for positions of prominence. One example of the results of such benefits is the Reverend E. V. Hill, who grew up in Sweet

Home and later gave the invocation at President Richard M. Nixon's inauguration in 1973.

The Slater Fund also contributed to the operation of county training schools in Texas, which offered schooling up to the eighth grade, plus vocational education. The General Education Board, created by an endowment from John D. Rockefeller, supported education for black students by paying the salaries of the state agents for Negro/Colored Schools as well as some teachers' salaries and by contributing to the construction of vocational training shops. The Jeanes Fund, established by Miss Anna T. Jeanes, a Quaker from Philadelphia, maintained a staff of pioneering black women who traveled throughout the state supporting teachers in rural black schools. The Jeanes teachers helped improve methods of instruction, introduced simple home industries, promoted sanitation and cleanliness, acquired libraries, and helped organize parent-teacher associations and Jeanes Clubs.

Samuel Walker Houston, the son of a slave owned by Texas legend Sam Houston, founded the Galilee School, later called Houstonian Normal and Industrial Institute, in Walker County with the help of these foundations. This school is a fine example of collaboration between black leaders and northern foundations to improve the lives of young African Americans. By 1928, four hundred students attended this school. The city of Huntsville, where Sam Houston's home is open for visitors today, recog-nized S. W. Houston's leadership by later naming a high school after him.

SCHOOLS FOR CHILDREN OF MEXICAN HERITAGE

While certainly some Spanish and Mexican children received academic instruction in Texas from the eighteenth century onward in various parts of the state, vast numbers of school-aged children of Mexican heritage only arrived with the advent of the 1910–1920 Mexican Revolution. Hundreds of thousands of Mexican refugees fled into Texas during the early decades of the twentieth century. Children who had experienced poverty, war, and destruction in their homeland entered one of the worst school systems in the United States when they crossed the border into Texas, according to Frederick Eby, Professor of Education at the University of Texas in the 1920s. Rural schools in Texas were poor compared to many other states' schools during this period. Eby claimed that most aspects of Texas education "were still in a disappointing and backward condition" in 1925. By his account, many of the essential problems of education in Texas remained unsolved since the Civil War:

After the labor of more than eighty years, and with the largest endowment for public education possessed by a single state in all the world, it is strange that education in Texas has not yet reached a satis-

factory basis and has not provided sufficiently for any one of the prime essentials.[5]

Many children of Mexican descent and generally low socioeconomic status attended schools in Texas that were poor by any standards. There were exceptions, of course, such as the Texas Mexican Industrial Institute near Kingsville, which opened in 1912, and the Presbyterian School for Mexican Girls in Taft, which opened in 1924. Children of Mexican heritage often had to work in the fields to help support their families, and they went to school only during cold or wet weather. Such children often migrated from farm to farm and from rural to urban settings throughout the year. Students of Mexican origin often started the school year late and left early. The effect of this migration was often referred to by white educators as "retardation," which meant being above the standard age for a certain grade level. In 1923–1924, 82 percent of the students in José Antonio Navarro Elementary School in San Antonio were over the average age for their grades. Children of Mexican heritage usually attended segregated schools during this time, even though there was no legal requirement for them to do so as there was for blacks. School buildings set aside for children of Mexican ancestry were generally poorly constructed, temporary structures that no longer exist today; however, some more solidly built schoolhouses remain in South Texas. Runn Elementary, which was built in 1901, still stands in the middle of the onion fields near Donna.

Professor H. T. Manuel of the University of Texas was one of the few professionals concerned with the problems of Spanish-speaking children in the first decades of the twentieth century. He concluded:

The most serious deficiency is in teaching and supervision. When we find a rural school with an untrained teacher—isolated, without vision, without equipment, and with a problem so great in teaching [Mexican immigrant children] that it challenges the most skilled—we have a most unhappy situation.[6]

School districts in San Antonio, El Paso, and the Lower Rio Grande Valley were leaders in developing innovative language approaches for Spanish-speaking children, but a progressive curriculum was rare for these students in most parts of the state. Emphasis was often on teaching oral English-language skills only, with reading, math, and other subjects totally neglected. "Americanization," or the de-culturation of

The Schoolhouse Morgue

The West Portland Schoolhouse, which no longer exists, once stood near the shore at White Point, near Corpus Christi. A powerful hurricane hit the coast on a September weekend in 1919 when hundreds of vacationers swarmed the beach. By Monday morning, bodies covered in black oil from the storage tanks at Port Aransas began to wash up at White Point. Rescue workers carried them to the schoolhouse, which was the largest building available in the vicinity. Later, many bodies were buried in mass graves before being moved to various places of final rest. Over one thousand people are estimated to have died in that storm.

"To have a second language is to have a second soul." This statement adorns the walls of Runn Elementary School near Donna in South Texas. The students' everyday experiences give truth to this message.

immigrant students common throughout the United States at this time, was a distinctive school theme. Even though the purpose of such a curriculum was to help immigrants blend into Anglo American life as quickly as possible, these tactics often had negative effects on non-English-speaking children, Hispanics as well as others. One elderly Norwegian American who grew up in Central Texas recalled that he often cried in frustration as a child when he was not allowed to speak his native Norwegian at school.

German Texans also suffered harassment concerning their language from time to time. During World War I, children in Central Texas were forbidden to speak German on the school grounds. To get around this, they would stick their heads through the fence and talk to each other in their native language. Thus, by their reasoning, they were off school grounds. Most of the original German textbooks in New Braunfels were put into storage during WWI and deteriorated beyond salvage.

Frederick Eby castigated the Texas educational system in 1925, saying:

The great trouble was that the people had been led to believe that the colossal permanent school fund was sufficient to take care of the entire educational needs of the state without resort to local taxation. This false belief which had come down from early times helped to keep the people in a state of apathy. Flattered by the boasts of office-seeking politicians that Texas had the largest school fund of the states in the world and that her schools were inferior to none, the people were living in complacent ignorance of the deplorable backwardness of the state school system. The majority of the people had no knowledge whatever of genuine standards of educational achievement.[7]

EXPANSION OF HIGHER EDUCATION

Despite Eby's criticism, during the early twentieth century, strides were made to increase academic opportunities, especially in terms of higher education. The Girls' Industrial College was founded in Denton in 1900 to educate young women of the state. The original name created a storm of protest, and citizens complained that it sounded like a reform school rather than an institution of higher learning. Letters to the trustees of the college derided the school and inquired about the "inmates." In an effort to improve public relations, the school catalog for the Girls' Industrial College protested, "This is not an orphanage, a hospital, or asylum, nor a reformatory. It is a high class school for the rich and poor alike, if they desire to attend and can meet the conditions for entrance." Denton already had a private normal school for training teachers, which shortly thereafter became North Texas State Normal School (now the University of North Texas). In 1905, the name of the female college was changed to the College of Industrial Arts. It later became the Texas State College for Women and, finally, Texas Woman's University in 1957.

The landmark Old Main, with its red, Gothic roof, was the first building erected on the campus of Southwest Texas State Normal School (now Texas State University) in 1903. The school's most famous student was Lyndon B. Johnson, who enrolled in 1927. LBJ worked his way through college by sweeping floors and helping in the university president's office. His education served him well when he was elected

Annie Webb Blanton taught English at North Texas State Normal School in Denton from 1901–1918. She was the first woman to win a statewide public office in Texas. After serving as state superintendent of public instruction, she ran unsuccessfully for United States Congress from Denton County in 1922.

to the United States Congress in 1937, where he served until becoming vice president of the United States in 1961. He became president in 1963 upon the death of John F. Kennedy and later led sweeping reforms in American education.

West Texas State Normal College (now West Texas A&M University) was founded in 1910 in Canyon after enthusiastic competition by over twenty-five towns for the school's location. The fact that Canyon had no saloons at the time may have played a role in the decision to locate the college there. Unfortunately, fire destroyed the classroom facilities four years after its founding. In an emotional appeal, the president of the school pledged to rebuild, saying that great institutions do not burn down. A new building with several classrooms, offices, a library, a swimming pool, and a gymnasium opened in 1916. The school also had a new faculty member that year, American painter Georgia O'Keefe. O'Keefe taught there for several years and was greatly influenced by the environment of the High Plains.

In 1911 Texas Christian University opened on the present campus in Fort Worth, and Southern Methodist University opened in Dallas. TCU began as Add-Ran Christian College, a small, private coeducational academy just west of Granbury, in the small community of Thorp Springs, in 1873. The site had two springs of clear water: one cold and sweet, and one sulfurous. Students would take a ritual swig from the sulfur spring, spit it out, and belch loudly. Texas is rich in college traditions, and this may be one of the first.

Rice Institute in Houston officially opened in 1912 after a sensational story of murder, betrayal, and intrigue unfolded. The university's benefactor, William Marsh Rice, was killed by his valet in 1900 in New York City as a result of the machinations of lawyer Albert T. Patrick. Patrick represented the heirs of Rice's second wife, who had died a few years previously. The heirs claimed half of the Rice fortune through a legal technicality. But Rice had long planned to use his wealth to establish a new university in Houston. Under Patrick's direction, the valet, Charles F. Jones, began to poison Rice slowly with mercury pills, but that soon proved too slow for the lawyer's taste. Patrick then obtained chloroform and instructed the valet to use it on Rice. Jones put the chloroformed rag over Rice's face as he slept in his bed, and the wealthy man simply never woke up. The two conspirators quickly tried to cash a check written on Rice's account. This scheme was foiled, however, because the valet misspelled Rice's name on the draft. Jones later

"There will be two holidays during the session, [one on] Christmas day and one in April. Parents will please not encourage nor expect their children to return home for Christmas, or any time until the close of school. It is impossible to have children do good work when they lose time from their studies."

Add-Ran Christian College catalog, 1883–1884

Wooden columns held up with supports mark the location of Add-Ran Christian College outside Granbury.

testified against Patrick at the trial, thus sending the crooked lawyer "up the river" to Sing Sing Prison in New York. To the benefit of Texas, the fortune was saved and Rice Institute founded.

Texas Technological College (now Texas Tech University) ushered in increasing intellectual challenges on the High Plains in 1925. More than nine hundred students chose training in agriculture, engineering, home economics or liberal arts at the spacious new Spanish Renaissance Revival campus that year. Embellishments and low-carved ornamentation highlight the administration building. Lubbock High School followed Northern Italian Romanesque styling a few years later to complement the Tech campus. The main entrance is surrounded with terracotta molding in panels representing various fields of study at the high school, such as drama, chemistry, homemaking, and athletics. The bell tower is characteristic of the architectural style and is topped with a weather vane sculpture of the Westerner, the school mascot.

In 1927, the Houston Independent School District took over a small school for black students that had its roots in the Houston Academy, started by Rev. John H. (Jack) Yates and other black pastors in 1885. As part of HISD, the school became a four-year college in 1935. Shortly after World War II, black postal worker Heman Marion Sweatt applied for admission to the University of Texas School of Law but was denied entrance on the basis of race. He then sued the university in the famous case *Sweatt v. Painter*. In response to this suit, the state hurriedly set up a law school exclusively for black students at the Houston facility, renaming the school Texas State University for Negroes (now Texas Southern University). The case then went to the Supreme Court, which ruled that all people must have equal access to educational facilities, thus opening the doors of once-segregated institutions of higher learning to all.

EDUCATION DURING THE DEPRESSION

The era of the Great Depression saw school resources contested in court, wealth lost as well as gained, terrible tragedy, and one of the greatest

periods of school construction in state history. One of the most important court cases was *Del Rio ISD v. Salvatierra*, which impacted Texas schools for decades. In 1930 Jesús Salvatierra and other Hispanic parents sued the Del Rio school board on the grounds that children of Mexican heritage were denied access to the higher-quality educational resources that white children enjoyed. The judge ruled in favor of the plaintiffs, but the case was overturned on appeal. The effect of this court of appeals ruling was to legalize segregation of Latino children in Texas schools until after World War II.

The 1930s saw many people, including Texas teachers and students, struggling to keep food on the table. Schools in many communities were forced to cut teachers' salaries, and more students than usual had to find jobs to help feed the family. One Mexican American woman who had to leave school in the 1930s recalled, "I cried and cried when I had to quit school. I didn't want to quit, but it was a matter of some of us not having enough to eat if I didn't." After sixth grade, she took a job washing clothes by hand on a scrub board for an Anglo family in town. Another Mexican American woman was luckier: the school actually gave her a job. When she

"To elevate the ideals, enrich the lives, and increase the capacity of the people for democratic self-government."

Senate Bill 103, 1923, on the purpose of establishing Texas Technological College in Lubbock

Ornate stonework at "Jeff" in San Antonio.

completed school in Taylor at sixteen, the school hired her as a caretaker. She swept the floors, lit the fire on cold days, and made soup for the children's lunch so they would get at least one meal a day.[8]

In East Texas, New London was one of the richest school districts in the United States at that time, and it was proud of the new multi-grade school completed in 1935. The structure was heated by raw gas from the nearby gas fields, as was common in that area. A blast ripped the building apart at about three o'clock on March 18, 1937, just at the end of the school day. The explosion buried the occupants in rubble and twisted steel with a force that was heard four miles away. Roughnecks rushed in from the oil fields, bringing heavy equipment to dig through the rubble. Texas Rangers and emergency crews worked frantically through the night. A thunderstorm blew in at about five o'clock the next morning, but still the desperate men worked. Morgues and hospitals in all surrounding towns filled to capacity, and many survivors needed treatment for shock and trauma. Almost all of the children from grades five through twelve in the town were injured or killed. Three hundred and eleven students and teachers died that day. In an amazing test of resilience and faith, the town rebuilt the school on the same location two years later. The state passed legislation that is still in force, mandating the addition of a distinctive odor to all gas for commercial or residential use so that people could be warned of a gas leak by the smell. A pink granite cenotaph, listing all the names of those who died in this sad event, stands in front of the rebuilt school today.

Also during the Depression, the ornate Thomas Jefferson High School was built in San Antonio in a climate of great financial disparity. Many people who had lost their jobs as a result of the economic downturn protested against this expensive project by the city. "Jeff" is perhaps the most architecturally elaborate school in the state. Built around two courtyards in Spanish Renaissance style, the building boasts extensive cast-stone detailing. The entrance is framed by a pair of domed towers modeled on Mexican Colonial counterparts. Columns at the entrance are reminiscent of stylized Maya carvings from southern Mexico. The library features a coffered ceiling embellished with oaken beams and brown and gold stenciling. Other innovations for the time included tile floors, built-in lockers, and indoor fire escapes.

Jeff opened its doors in the winter of 1932, and graduated its first class that spring with Gus Garcia as the first valedictorian. Years later, as an attorney, he filed the landmark lawsuit *Delgado v. Bastrop ISD* (1948), which ended the segregation of children of Mexican descent in Texas schools brought about by *Del Rio ISD v. Salvatierra*. In 1937, a survey by the United Press of fifteen hundred schools nationwide declared Thomas Jefferson High School the most outstanding school in the United States. *LIFE* magazine put Jeff on the cover in March 1938, and several Hollywood movies were filmed there.

"We rode the wagon when I first started. The wagon came about five miles to pick up kids. That was 1931. The man who drove that wagon would never trot those horses. I thought we would never get there, especially during bad weather."

C. D. Garrison, Matador, Texas

CONCLUSION

Education in Texas moved from the log cabin to the most modern facilities in the country in the one hundred years from the 1830s to the 1930s. Notions of curriculum were expanded and changed to reflect new necessities such as vocational education, business training, modern languages, and advanced mathematics. Opportunities for black and Mexican American students widened, as they did for handicapped students and others. Women and girls continued to be active in all phases of schooling, as they had from the earliest days. Universities were built, and old institutions fell away. Without a doubt, education opened the door to a more prosperous life for many Texans.

Teaching school was also a vehicle for advancement for a variety of prominent Texans. Sam Rayburn, Speaker of the U.S. House of Representatives from 1940 to 1961, taught in Greenwood and several small schools in Fannin County to pay his way through East Texas Normal College in Commerce. Historian Walter Prescott Webb imparted basic academic skills to children in various small Texas schools before heading for the University of Texas. President Lyndon B. Johnson followed in his father's and great-grandfather's footsteps by teaching at Welhausen School in Cotulla in 1928 and later in Houston. Ann Richards taught history at Fulmore Middle School in 1956 in Austin before becoming the first woman since Annie Webb Blanton elected to statewide office as state treasurer in 1982. She later became governor of the state in 1990.

In the twenty-first century, Texas continues to grapple with issues of school financing, curriculum, increased high school rigor, and the expansion of higher education, reflecting our changing economic needs and social attitudes. This brief history of schooling in Texas has omitted various aspects important to education, such as the details of administration and state regulation, and instead has focused on the social history of schools across the state as illustrated by the school buildings themselves. Many other stories can certainly be told. From modest one-room schoolhouses to the grandest institutions, schools have developed and changed to serve the people. Diverse ideas about education in Texas will continue to direct the destiny of the state's children as needs for new kinds of learning emerge.

"Teaching was the hardest work I had ever done, and remains the hardest work I have done to date."

Ann Richards

1. Head Start is an educational program for pre-kindergarten children that began under President Lyndon B. Johnson in 1965.

2. Indianola was selected by colonizer Prince Carl of Solms-Braunfels as the entry port for German colonists in Texas. The bustling port, which was located in Calhoun County near present-day Port Lavaca, was destroyed by a catastrophic hurricane on September 16, 1875.

3. Rincon Street is now known as N. St. Mary's Street.

4. The vast majority of public schools in Texas did not integrate black and white students until the Elementary and Secondary Education Act of 1965 gave them financial incentive to do so.

5. Eby, F. 1925. *The Development of Education in Texas*. New York: Macmillan, p. 304.

6. Manuel, H. T. 1930. *The Education of Mexican and Spanish-Speaking Children in Texas*. Austin: The University of Texas Press, p. 60.

7. Eby, F. 1925. *The Development of Education in Texas*. New York: Macmillan, p. 218.

8. Black, M. S. 1996. *Historical Factors Affecting Mexican American Parental Involvement and Educational Outcomes: The Texas Environment from 1910–1996*. Dissertation. Cambridge, MA: Harvard University, p. 205.

Information for this book was gathered from a number of sources, including several primary source Internet sites. To begin the process of locating old school buildings in Texas, we relied on the online Texas Historic Sites Atlas *from the Texas Historical Commission, which contains the full text from all state historical markers, county by county, plus the full text of registration materials for buildings and places on the National Register of Historic Places. The detailed county road maps from* The Roads of Texas *(1999) by Shearer Publishing in Fredericksburg, Texas, were also extremely helpful for locating existing buildings and ruins as we crossed the state and photographed many isolated locations. We also relied extensively on the Handbook of Texas Online from the Texas State Historical Association for facts concerning individuals, institutions, and the general context of the development of schooling in Texas. Useful books and articles were also consulted. In addition, whenever a date for the founding of Texas colleges and universities was in question (which was often), we opted for the date listed on the institutions' official Web sites. Finally, we thank the many individuals who shared with us their personal recollections about going to school in Texas.*

Bay, Debby. 1976. "The Shaping of Texas Public Schools." *Texas Outlook* 60 (March/April).

Eby, Frederick. 1925. *The Development of Education in Texas.* New York: Macmillan.

Fisher, Alice and James D. 1986. "Common Schools of Central Texas: Past and Present (one and two room schools of the Hill Country)." *Heritage IV,* (II), pp. 23, 37–41. Texas Historical Foundation.

Gillespie County Program Building Committee. 1983. *Gillespie County School Histories.* Fredericksburg, TX: Dietel and Son Printing.

Green, Stan. 1990. *Schools in Early Laredo. The Story of Laredo.* Laredo, TX: Texas A&M International University.

Manuel, Herschel T. 1930. *The Education of Mexican and Spanish-Speaking Children in Texas.* Austin: The University of Texas Press.

Roads of Texas, The. 1999. Fredericksburg, TX: Shearer Publishing.

WEB SITES

Huston-Tillotson University. http://www.htu.edu

Texas A&M University. http://www.tamu.edu.

Texas Historical Commission. Texas Historic Sites Atlas. http://atlas.thc.state.tx.us.

Texas State Historical Association. The Handbook of Texas Online. http://www.tsha.utexas.edu/handbook/online.

Texas Tech University. http://www.ttu.edu.

The University of Texas. http://www.utexas.edu.

Wiley College. http://www.wileyc.edu.

EAST TEXAS

Palestine High School, which opened in 1916 in Palestine, is noted for its
Jacobean brickwork and fine architecture. The building currently serves as
a museum of community history.

Auditorium at Palestine High School.

Maintenance man with an original heat boiler in Palestine High School.

All that remains of Lincoln High School, a two-story Rosenwald school for African American students in Palestine, are overgrown steps and the faint footprint of the foundation.

Neighborhood resident explains how the Lincoln High School burned in 1995.

Abandoned slide across from the remains of the Lincoln High School in Palestine.

The Ratcliff Rosenwald School is currently used as a fellowship building for the small country church in the pines of Houston County.

clockwise from top right: Churches and Rosenwald schools were often the centers of black communities; a former Ratcliff student checks on the building frequently; former students live near the Ratcliff School.

Pine Grove Rosenwald School in Cherokee County.

The Marshall Rosenwald School building is currently used as a private home.

Some old Rosenwald school buildings are difficult to recognize due to extensive remodeling over the years. This building in Cass County is currently used as a church hall.

Playground at the West Point Rosenwald School in Gregg County.

An overgrown children's playground at the old Garland Community
Rosenwald School, located on former plantation land.

Mrs. Jenna Benton, a former student of the Garland Community School in Bowie County,
and her nephew, Lorenzo "Pete" Shavers, inspect the abandoned teacherage her family
lived in when the school closed. Mrs. Benton's grandmother was a slave on the Garland
plantation, and many of her descendents remain in the area.

Students pose in front of the W. D. Spigner School in Calvert, which was built with Rosenwald funds.

Children's laughter is no longer heard at the old Lockhart Rosenwald School.

Lockhart Vocational High School is an example of a two-story Rosenwald school.
The school closed in the 1960s when Lockhart schools integrated. The building
was then used as a Head Start Center for several years.

Simple privies were the only option for students and faculty of the
Sweet Home Rosenwald School.

Sweet Home was a Rosenwald school located just outside Seguin. Like many
Rosenwald schools, it is now used as a community center.

The Freedmen's Aid Society of the Methodist Episcopal Church founded
Wiley College in Marshall, Texas, for African Americans in 1873.

The president's house at Wiley College.

Wiley College Administration Building.

"I used to ride by here by myself on

horseback when I was seven or eight

years old. The rumor was that the

cemetery was haunted, so I was scared

to death."

—Seventy-year-old Floyd "Bunkie" Meutch
on riding to the Young School House
and Cemetery near Smithville

Floyd and Helen Meutch grew up near the Young School House.

Floyd and Helen visit old friends at the Young School House Cemetery next to the school.

The Young School House, built in 1872 in Bastrop County, has been used as
a church for many years.

A ghostly window at Mary Allen whispers the hopes and dreams of the
black students who studied there.

The old administration building of Mary Allen Seminary in Crockett stands in ruins today.
At one time, the campus had twelve buildings, dormitories, a fountain, and landscaped gardens.

Mary Allen doorway.

clockwise from top right: Overgrown gardens and fountain at Mary Allen; obscured signpost to the future at Mary Allen; forgotten steps to a better life at Mary Allen.

Detail of a doorknob in the building at Tehuacana.

The original building of Trinity University is located in the community of Tehuacana, northeast of Waco in Limestone County. The building is now used as a religious retreat center.

Tehuacana with the old bell tower in the background. The tower has been removed for restoration. It stands between 20–30 feet tall and is intricately constructed.

Texas A&M University in College Station was the first state-supported institution
of higher education for white students in Texas.

Blinn College in Brenham was organized in 1883. The pink main building with clock tower dates from 1906.

The American flag was flying high even though the school last held class in 1965.

Like many schools in small communities, the Sharp School was a WPA project. It is a large brick school with an intricate façade, built in the early 1940s.

In 1951 Gene Luckey taught science and physical education, and coached basketball. "I coached many a game here. Over there is the front entrance to the gym. Back there was the back entrance."

The steps are still there but the gym is now a large garden.

"Back there was the kitchen where the students ate. And that building is where they learned about agriculture and welding.

"Back there, where the pond is, was a building for the GI center. That was where the soldiers were taught things so they could try and make a living after they came home from WWII.

"The [main] building was built to hold five hundred students. When the war came, a lot of folks moved to the city to work in the plants or they enlisted and never came back. A lot has changed. But folks are again moving into the county. They want to raise their kids in smaller communities. We may need to re-open this building."

Sharp School in Milam County.

Gene Luckey now owns the Sharp School building, where he once taught.

Like many older schools, the roof on the Sharp School has collapsed in a lot of places. When that happens, the rest of the building slowly goes with it, which seems to be a metaphor for the communities themselves.

"A big part of the problem in the county is the water supply. There's not enough water to support the people. There used to be a lot of small communities. There were big families every one hundred to two hundred acres. You had a lot of schools because you had to be able to walk or ride a horse to school back then. You couldn't go much further. There were a lot of one- and two-room schoolhouses all over.

"Up until five or ten years ago you could drive thirty miles and hardly see a house. Not anymore."

Mr. Luckey moved to Rockdale when the school closed and continued to teach and coach. He kept coming back to Sharp and working on the land he now owns, behind the Sharp School. He had over three hundred trees in a peach orchard but the drought got them.

"Go down to San Gabriel. There's an old school there, petrified wood for the stones. There's no roof, only the walls are left."

Mr. Luckey now owns the Sharp School building.

The interior of the New London High School in Rusk County exhibits tile
floors and original light fixtures from 1939.

Trophy case at New London High School.

The school in New London was reconstructed after a horrific
explosion killed 311 students and teachers in 1937.

Window at Gaston School, near Henderson in Rusk County.

New towns sprang up in the gas fields of East Texas during the 1920s as profits poured in from oil. The magnificent school at Gaston, completed in 1932, sits alone, the town no longer in existence.

CENTRAL TEXAS

The German Free School in Austin started in 1852 as a private German-language school.

The Albert School at Williams Creek in Gillespie County is one of twelve remaining one-room country schools preserved in that county that were started by German immigrants.

Child's swing at Pecan Creek School in Gillespie County.

Often two students shared one desk at the Pecan Creek School in Gillespie County. The mark down the middle separates "my side" from "your side."

Desks of different sizes for students of different sizes at Pecan Creek School.

Former students return to their childhood school in Gillespie County.

Exterior of Pecan Creek School.

The cut-stone Morris Ranch School was built for the children of the ranch hands in 1893 in Gillespie County and continued its operation until 1962, when it merged with Fredericksburg schools. The building is currently a private home.

Pease Elementary School in Austin began as a public free school in 1876.

Interior of the old school in Oatmeal, which is now used as a church.

The one-room, limestone school building at Oatmeal in
Burnet County was erected in 1869.

Children's feet leave a worn path that

echoes the shape of a merry-go-round

like a shadow from the noon sun.

Merry-go-round at Okhalla School.

Okhalla School in Burnet County now serves as a community center.

The painted stage drop in Okhalla demonstrates business support of local schools during the 1920s–1930s.

The two-story, red brick elementary school in Bertram, Burnet County, opened in the fall of 1909 and still serves the children of the area.

Foundation of the Union Hill Consolidated School in Bosque County.

The abandoned Mosheim School in Bosque County.

Detail of Georgetown High School.

This Spanish Colonial Revival building was constructed in 1924 as the high school for Georgetown in Williamson County. It still serves students today as an elementary school.

Original fire escapes at Granger High School from the 1920s.

Granger High School reflects the architectural style popular
in the mid-1920s, when it was built.

"We may have been poor,
but we were rich in spirit."

Dr. Bill Orman, on the Lampasas
Colored School, where he served as principal
for twenty years. Today, Dr. Orman is a professor
at Prairie View A&M University.

Dr. Bill Orman of Prairie View A&M was the principal of Lampasas Colored
School during the 1950s and early 1960s. Prairie View was the first state-
supported institute of higher education for African Americans in Texas.

Pressed-tin ceiling of the Lampasas Colored School. Additions such as indoor toilets were made in 1948. Until 1951, black students could only go as far as tenth grade in Lampasas. Some students lived with relatives in cities such as San Antonio to complete all ten grades.

Detail of Lampasas Colored School.

The two-room stone building of the Lampasas Colored School, constructed in 1923, is not a Rosenwald school. Instead, funds for construction were raised by local citizens with school bonds. Classes continued here until 1963, when schools integrated.

Cornerstone and pavilion at Add-Ran Christian College in Hood County.
The school was named for two brothers, Addison and Randolph Clark, who
founded the institution in 1873.

Fulmore Middle School opened in Austin in 1886; the present building dates back to the early twentieth century. Ann Richards taught here before becoming governor of Texas.

Students pursued courses leading to a teaching certificate at San Fernando Academy, which was established in Pontotoc in Mason County in 1883. After the original academy failed in Pontotoc, the building was used as a public school until 1927.

Peeling walls and blackboard inside Briggs High School.

Broken window at Briggs High School.

The roof caved in on this part of the high school in Briggs, Burnet County. About four hundred students graduated from Briggs High School from 1919 to 1964, when the high school program was transferred to Florence. Vines appear to hold the old walls together today.

Doorway at Briggs High School.

The auditorium at Briggs High School is still in use.

The old gym at the San Gabriel School.

The San Gabriel School in Williamson County was built by the Works Progress Administration (WPA).

The star-shaped fountain at the Clairette School was added by WPA workers.

A new recreation building for the Clairette School District was built by the WPA school in Erath County.

The two-story, native stone Clairette schoolhouse in Erath County opened in 1912 and continued its educational function until 1949. Since then it has been used as a community center and polling place.

Foundation posts of the old gym sit like headstones in a cemetery at the deteriorated Clairette School.

"A cultivated mind is the

guardian genius of democracy."

Mirabeau B. Lamar, second president
of the Republic of Texas, 1839

Constructed in 1904, The Dorothy Gebauer Building is the oldest
building on the UT campus. The Will C. Hogg Building is on the right.

The creation of the University of Texas at Austin completed Mirabeau B. Lamar's
dream of two state-supported universities for Texas.

Battle Hall across UT's main plaza was constructed in 1911 in Mediterranean Renaissance style as the university library.

UT's Sutton Hall was completed in 1916 as the College of Education.

The white limestone Gothic building at St. Edward's University in Austin opened in 1903.

Archway at St. Edward's University.

Stonework at St. Edward's University.

The interior of the main building at St. Edward's University.

Metz Elementary School, Austin. Metz was built in 1916 to serve the expanding student enrollment that resulted from the Compulsory School Act of 1915 at the beginning of World War I. The new building dates from 1992.

SOUTH TEXAS

Carvings in the stone at the old Ursuline Academy.

Statue at Ursuline.

Ursuline Academy, which opened in 1851, sits on the bank of the River Walk in San Antonio. Classes at the Catholic school were held at this location for 115 years.

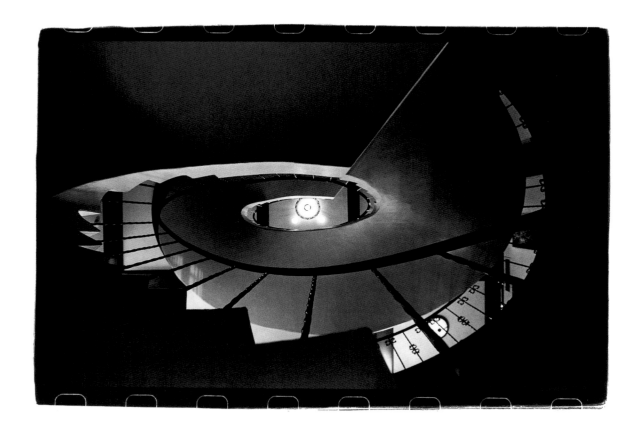

An old stairwell at St. Mary's Institute leads guests upstairs in a River Walk hotel.

In 1853, St. Mary's Institute opened in this location on the San Antonio River as a school for boys. Today, the remains of the building have been incorporated into a luxury hotel.

Central Catholic High School in San Antonio began as St. Mary's Institute in 1852.
Central Catholic may be the oldest continuously operating school in Texas.
The present building dates from 1932.

Chapel at Central Catholic High School.

Brother Richard Martens, Glee Club director at Central Catholic High School for over twenty years.

Shooting competition at Central Catholic.

Brother Martens's hands and songbook at Central Catholic.

The four-story, Gothic main building of Our Lady of the Lake University in San Antonio opened in 1896.

Our Lady of the Lake University in San Antonio began when the Sisters of Divine Providence opened a girls' school in 1896. College-level courses began in 1911.

Entrance hall of the main building at Our Lady of the Lake.

Stairway in the main hall of Our Lady of the Lake.

Footprints at Bonham Elementary.

Bonham Elementary, built in 1889, is still in use today in San Antonio.

The old Fourth Ward School in San Antonio (1875) now serves as the Administration Building for San Antonio Independent School District.

Children slid down the fire escapes during fire drills at the Frederick Douglass School in San Antonio.

The Frederick Douglass School in San Antonio became the first junior high school in Texas for black children.

The opulence of Thomas Jefferson High School in San Antonio created controversy
when it opened in 1932.

The Welhausen School (in the background) sits across the plaza from the
park in Cotulla, where Lyndon B. Johnson taught as a young man.

The much-remodeled Head Start Center sits across the street from the Catholic church and seminary in Hebbronville. Don Bonifacio Garza originally built this dwelling with adobe brick and a grass roof in 1893. Much later, the building was used as a private school, which conducted its classes in Spanish for over twenty years.

159

"It shall be his duty to guard the

conduct of the children both in and

out of school, making them understand

in a clear manner the veneration and

respect they owe to the public authorities,

their parents, old persons, and elders;

also that they shall be careful with the

cleanliness of speech, deportment, and

good conduct."

Laredo City Council, 1821, on approving
schoolmaster José Lázaro Benavides

Old Laredo High School looks over the Rio Grande. Built in 1916, the structure now serves as a hotel in downtown Laredo.

The school board for Laredo Independent School District meets in this restored church
building from the early twentieth century in the St. Peter's district, not far from downtown.

Amid the fragrance of huisache and orange trees, Laredo ISD offices in the St. Peter's
district of the city utilize buildings that were once private homes during the late 1800s.

Laredo Community College at Ft. McIntosh.

Laredo Community College was established on the grounds of historic Fort McIntosh in 1946. Ft. McIntosh was founded around 1850, and many of the buildings used today date from the 1880s.

St. Augustine Parochial School on the main plaza in Laredo was built in 1927.

Children scramble on the old parade ground of Ft. Ringgold in Rio Grande City.

Rio Grande City schools are housed in the buildings of Ft. Ringgold,
a decommissioned army post dating from 1848.

Children often sit in the shade on this bench near the Manuel Guerra Building in Roma.

For many years, children of Mexican heritage had to look through the fence at white-only schools. Today, the Manuel Guerra Building is open to all as part of the public schools in Roma.

The Hidalgo ISD Administration Building, constructed in 1898, sits near the Rio Grande on the Mexican border. The building has been a place of learning, but also of refuge from hurricanes and floods for more than one hundred years.

Rich land along the Rio Grande still draws families to the area near
Runn Elementary (in the background).

Donna Central Elementary School stands like a fortress, a symbol of the
importance of education in the community.

John Mendoza with his daughter Andrea in front of Donna Central Elementary School.
Mr. Mendoza went to school in this building as a child and later became the school's principal.

Pitted interior walls of Tuleta Grade School.

Tuleta Grade School.

Tuleta Grade School in Bee County was built by the WPA during the Great Depression.

Standing in the overgrown brush, the Normanna School had several rooms, including a multi-purpose room to be used as a classroom, lunchroom, and auditorium—complete with stage and sliding doors. But it only had eleven grades.

The door to nowhere at old Yoakum High.

Like the quiet after the battle, the WPA high school building in Yoakum,
Dewitt County, sits alone.

WEST TEXAS

West Texas is so expansive it defies imagination. That is why legends are born. Langtry, home of "the law west of the Pecos" and Judge Roy Bean, is known, now, in stories and old movies. But Langtry isn't a legend; it is real. Great ranches were carved out of the hard land on the northern edge of the Chihuahuan Desert where Native Americans lived thousands of years ago, leaving pictographs on the rock walls hidden among the canyons that have been cut by the Rio Grande.

Today, a few families live in Langtry, but the school has been closed and is now used as a community center. Children, the few that still live in the area, must go to school in Comstock, miles away.

The Langtry schoolhouse overlooks the canyons along the Rio Grande, west of Del Rio.

The adobe-brick schoolhouse at Terlingua near Big Bend sits abandoned amid the cactus. Scholars were shaded only by a tent from 1907 to 1929 until this building was constructed around 1930.

School for children of Mexican descent in Marathon, Brewster County.

The door of Marathon Mexican School.

Mrs. Johnnie Chambers, matriarch of the school

and the land at the end of the road in the Big Bend.

She had been the first woman to work on an oil drilling

crew as a mud-logger in Montana in her younger days.

Mrs. Chambers—Johnnie—was a teacher for over

thirty years for all children, from both sides of the

river, who came to her classroom door.

Schoolchildren in Candelaria can only attend this school through the eighth grade.
They must ride the bus more than forty miles each way to attend high school.

Johnnie Chambers taught for thirty-five years in this school in Candelaria,
at the end of the road in Presidio County. The original part of the building is
more than one hundred years old.

U.S. Army wives taught post children on Officers' Row at Ft. Davis after the Civil War.

As the children grew in number, the school moved to the post chapel at Ft. Davis,
which guarded the Butterfield Stage Trail during the 1800s.

The abandoned Whiteflat School sits silently in Motley County.

The community of Whiteflat, north of Lubbock,

disappeared in the dust of the thirties, run out by

the Depression. Cotton gins, gas stations, stores.

Almost all of it. The brick shell of the school and

the remains of a gas station are all that is left.

Shades of vocational education in Whiteflat.

Interior of Ivy Chapel and School.

A cross and a windmill watch over Ivy Chapel and School built in Kimble County in 1917.

The curtain is open at Valley View, revealing the set for the last theater production. Figures are still fresh, but the play is long over.

Valley View Rural High School was built by the WPA in Cottle County.

MARY BLACK

Mary Black has taught in Texas public schools and at the University of Texas at Austin. She holds a doctorate from Harvard University's Graduate School of Education and currently consults on education around the country. She grew up in Denton, Texas, where her grandfather moved his family in 1925 so that all the kids could go to college. She has one son, Miles, and is married to an archeologist who knows Texas better than anybody. She and her husband Steve live in Austin and swim almost every day in the cold waters of Barton Springs.

BRUCE JORDAN

Bruce Jordan is a documentary photographer and occasionally an educator. Born in Dallas, Bruce has traveled across the state, photographing and meeting folks. His first book (with Craig Hillis), *Texas Trilogy: Life in a Small Texas Town*, was taken from the Steven Fromholz folk song of the same name, and was also published by UT Press. Bruce has one son, Caleb, who has no intention of following in his father's footsteps.

INDEX

Requests for permission to reproduce material
from this work should be sent to:
    Permissions
    University of Texas Press
    P.O. Box 7819
    Austin, TX 78713-7819
    www.utexas.edu/utpress/about/bpermission.html

The paper used in this book meets the minimum
requirements of ANSI/NISO Z39.48-1992 (R1997)
(Permanence of Paper).

LIBRARY OF CONGRESS CATALOGING-IN-PUBLICATION DATA

Black, Mary S., 1946–
  Early Texas schools : a photographic history /
text by Mary S. Black ; photographs by Bruce Jordan. — 1st ed.
      p. cm.
  Includes bibliographical references and index.
  ISBN 978-0-292-71733-6 (alk. paper)
  1. Education—Texas—History. I. Jordan, Bruce F., 1953–
II. Title.
  LA370.B53 2008
  370.9764'09034—dc22   2007020256

Cameras: Canon EOS 1N
Lenses: EF 20-35 f2.8L
           EF 35 f2
           EF 85 f1.8
           EF 200 f2.8L
Film: Ilford HP5
Paper: Ilford Multigrade IV RC Pearl
Lighting: Available light

The typeface used in this book is Scala, designed by Martin
Majoor and released in 1993. Trained as a book designer and
typographer, he designed this typeface and its companion sans
serif and named them after the Teatro alla Scala in Milan. The
designs are based in the humanist tradition of typefaces such
as Bembo and Fournier, with low contrast and strong serifs.

Book design by Lisa C. Tremaine